AF484012

# FIRE IN YOUR VOICE

Collected Poems

Tierra Montgomery

Copyright

© 2022  Tierra Montgomery

# OTHER WORKS

flowers
HOMELAND
IF FREEDOM HAD A NAME
One Month That Gave Me Rebirth

# FIRE IN YOUR VOICE

Collected Poems

Tierra Montgomery

# TABLE OF CONTENTS

# TABLE OF CONTENTS

# TABLE OF CONTENTS

# TABLE OF CONTENTS

# Voices That Consume World

Does one hear them?
But not see them?

Does one trace their voices?
Know the way or why?

Sat in a home, in a car
Trickling down speeds of sweat.

Can not bear minding their voices.
Can not bear one more time.

And just one time for them to stop speaking.
And just one time to not surprise me.

It is not a birthday.
But a slow rupture of screams waiting to happen.

Anywhere but in mind.
Anywhere but there.

# Exhausted

Time beats mind over again.
Sending shockwave after shockwave.

Questions go unanswered.
Why is this happening?

Do not understand.
Mind always racing.

# As Love Stories Will  Be

What love opens doors, shatters,
Surfaces, resurfaces, has an epiphany.

What love forms in crevices of words,
Molds together beauty, leaves heartache.

What ways we interact with love,
Not being in love, out of love, loving again.

How is it we communicate?
In translations, lost in translations.

How actions form a harmony.
To say without saying.

The intentions that hold invisible lines.
Invisible standards.

Invisible expectations.
Invisible words that speak the loudest.

But there is love between communicating and interactions.
How they dance together.

Sometimes tripping over expectations and standards.
Sometimes falling out of love with one another.

Sometimes leaning forward into each other.
And we too, play in this dance.

Devising  between self and norms.
Refuting between standards and expectations.

When communication and interactions do not work out.
When the invisible becomes visible

When everything breaks loose.
When nothing makes sense.

Why does love feel it should leave?
Why does love break?

# Internal Voice

Grit teeth.
Backbiting words.

What words seep internally.
Childhood lays a foundation.

But relearning shines above a crescent moon.
Unworthiness.

Whose unworthy?
Not one.

Rooted in shame,
Breaks glass, speaking into the void.

Not scared of fear anymore.
Shakes no more furry.

Dysfunction once held its place.
Now upheaval.

Now listen.
Now see.

See what is brewing internally.
See what new beliefs have become.

Seems simple enough.
But even seams pop open after years of tears.

This worth pops up after years of tears.
Perhaps this voice breaks sometimes.

Perhaps it broke into a voice more courageous.
Something worth screaming about.

# In A Sovereign State

Maps outline escape routes across body.
Make landmarks where eyes should go.

Is there ever one way of seeing this iniquity?
Eyes bore bloodshed tears.

Cries scream names of the ones not breathing.
Places become beacons of warning.

Beats chest in furry
Uncertain, yet bounded.

And pen scratches notes filled with lost "love you(s)"
Lost smiles.

The hope for tomorrow sinking into quicksand.
There nothing stays.

To ever wonder what longed for behind hurt skin.
Hurt mouth.

Hurt piling on top of hurt.
Hurt never releasing its hold.

Generations growing up speaking the same language.
Our bodies crumble.

Wither away the escape routes.
The asphalt cracks at the seams.

And it seems that is what this shaped to be.
Being an ever present worry.

An ever present bundle of scrutiny.
What loud voices bang on the door.

Waiting to be heard.
Wanting to feel seen, to be understood.

Landmarks become replaced with something new.
Something once remembered turned forgotten.

To be forgotten.
How can everything change and still be the same?

# Not Perfection

Perfection creases the corners of mind.
Makes its way down the spine.

Shivers.
What more could perfection be?

That love was perfect?
To have perfection is to love?

No.
Nothing is ever perfect.

Not rooted in an ever present fear.
Not rooted in shame.

To love oneself like this,
Is to not accept beating oneself up.

# Of What Beauty

This speck of hope,
Lead to frustrations than to clarity

Whose standards are I going by?
Because they do not feel like my own.

Pivot.
Pivot from love to lackluster

Something barely understood.
Something not exercised.

Something frustrating.
But where did this voice go?

The one with strongness.
The one with conviction.

And is it not that writing stems from many experiences?
From personal to other places?

And where is my place?
Mind a gurgling mess.

Afraid to lose a voice just found.
So where is the excitement?

Where is the flow accustomed too?
Has it left?

And am now stuck.
In a decision can not seem to resolve.

To heal.
To find a place in the sea of what things mean.

Of what there is truly to be said.
And there is fear.

# Raspy Winters

We speak of traditions as the Earth sculpts another human.
Another berry.

Another tragedy.
Picking the remnants of a fractured history.

Telling stories over hot coco.
Which histories captivates minds.

What other countries and cultures learn.
Learn in the wake of what we produce.

Each generation learns something new.
Something that becomes a part of the culture.

It is like what is said in Sociology,
To be built as a part of a community.

To be built as part of social learning.
What words we weld together.

What makeup we paint with our interpretations.
Creasing each letter, each emotion.

We built a forest of humanity.
Not contrived by absences of what-ifs.

Not contrived by past transgressions.
But in awe of healing oneself.

In awe of learning new traditions.
Of creating new histories.

Of leaning into what we can strive for,
And not into what holds us back.

# Affirmations

Love.
What a worthwhile expression.

Believe.
To ensure self.

To make certain.
A purpose worth living.

Preparing the road ahead.
A longing yet to be discovered.

# Traveling Asphalt

Crisp edges neatly fall in line.
Hits asphalt beats the break of time.

Seemingly where has time gone.
What due diligence we hold onto.

Capturing the sound of birds squawking,
Flying in the air.

What summer's day brings.
But joy and tranquility.

Marveling at where everyone goes.
To the lake, to a restaurant, to home

Marveling at why we move the way we move.
To church, to garden, to sing.

Singing different emotions, different sounds.
Different people coming together to form a unit.

What does going away and being together mean?
What does it mean to stay in a place we call home?

And if it meant solitude or a group of people,
Why must there be a difference?

Where is the balance in this traveling?
Traveling where and with whom?

Traveling when and why?
Traveling against perceptions.

Painting a canvas of beginnings.
Knowing there will be a destination.

Knowing there will be an end,
A forever awakening.

# Scuffle

Scraped knees, crying in the distance.
Mother coos and soothes the aching child.

Wrestles with a band-aid,
A smile to cheer up the child.

Wrestles with many mornings,
A time to wake up and get ready.

But not just for herself.
But with a child in toe.

And the little one, not knowing the worry.
Not knowing the angst sometimes the world bleeds.

But only knowing the love a mother gives.
The love that seeps from "I love you(s)" to cozy hugs.

Some say that there is beauty in eyes.
But there is also beauty in one's soul.

Break against a hard shell.
Weeps for the little one and what is set forth in the world.

Weeps of possible pains.
Weeps of possible goods.

This life scuffles with everything in it.
But a mother's love is a nice band-aid.

# What Wonders

Eyes that could not see.
Ears that could not hear.

The way imagery is used,
And wondered how to still convey a message.

Understanding to the tune of someone else.
What atmospheres draw on us, resonate with us.

What worlds shape us, make us believe in these worlds.
And in an aperture, hands drawn to one another,

Let us reign in empathy.
Let us live in unity.

# Bring Us Into Your World

Hearing Cadence.
Calls outside of rooms.

Brightly lit hallways.
Calls while walking.

Never knowing when,
The next voice bigger than the last.

Sings in rhymes not recognized.
In rhythms that beat to a tune not known.

Calls a few seconds after waking
What blaring alarm clock the mind can make.

Calls whenever Cadence please,
When Cadence must.

Dials freely in mind
Yet hears Cadence as an outside voice.

Like someone speaking far away, screaming.
Wanting to be heard.

Wanting the edges of buildings to fold into itself.
Wanting to believe.

Believe that every word is true.
Believe that every instance was not fictitious.

The words dip into reality.
Riding the waves of sanity.

Course after course,
Sending alert signals to core.

Could hear man, woman.
Could hear any time of night or day.

But could not place when
Could not place where

Just knew at some moment Cadence was coming.
Knew the scarcity of mind dwindled.

# Validity

Traces lines in the sand.
Pounds a basketball against asphalt.

Wondering now if any of it was real.
Trigger words.

Words that call into suspect.
Words that lead to many questions.

Questions own validity.
Where is the security?

Why be not believed?
Why not see what each other sees?

# Wayward Whimsy

Side eyeing medicines.
What would work for the brain?

What would not cause conniptions.
Or lead to more hallucinations.

How did medicine help?
Gives lost serotonin.

Relieves depression.
But watch out for how the body responds.

Each medicine works in different ways.
Some have a strong dosage.

Some make one sleepy.
Some interact with other medicines.

How scary this can be.
But when the right one comes along.

All is right with the world.
No frustrations.

No hallucinations.
One balanced world.

# Loving Self Through Process

Coils like a snake.
Gives warning signs.

Bites when feeling threatened.
And felt threatened.

By what these medicines will do.
Felt what was wrong with oneself?

Sometimes to get to a normal,
One must learn a new way of seeing.

Finding a new viewpoint.
Finding a new perspective.

Had to accept where this road leads.
Had to accept a new normal.

# Aren't We All Listening

Landscapes make great photographs.
There is something majestic in the way a mate is calling.

Calls in a burly voice or
Calls in high pitched tones or

Lets silence speak.
Place hands across grains of sand.

Wisps of clouds spread their wings across the sky.
Is there any wonder why Earth's beauty can be so serene?

# An Opening

Gateways to a wonder in a time.
Fought lies, got grit skin.

Sink into the belly of uncomfortability.
What lies beneath these feet.

A tortured expression.
Staring back with hate.

Staring back with a lost face.
Lost words.

Just being lost.
Guess this means we are both lost.

But in different ways.
Struggling to find harmony.

The harmony that sits in hearts.
A connection of understanding.

And when will there be understanding?
When will there be peace?

# Care

Embarking on this journey.
Towards love for oneself.

A step forward in the right direction.
A direction to lean into what makes you, you.

When time seems to dwindle,
What time is there to carve for oneself?

Being intentional to sculpt out time.
Being mindful to develop skills.

A destination worth arriving too.
A home worth building.

Sometimes days and nights merge together.
Sometimes life can be too much to bear.

In essence, the process long.
Grueling at what may encounter.

You are worth the time.
You are worth what it takes.

# Something Amazing

No longer a distorted lens
Whose eyes do not furry

To nurture a gift.
To learn to build armor.

To begin to heal in life.
Not rushing the process.

Allowing being present to take hold.
To foster into a new habit.

Stampedes on self-doubt, self-destruction.
We are built to love.

Especially loving ourselves.
Life is not linear.

Not a one-fits-all recipe.
With many different ways to begin.

Identifying the strengths
Licking wounds to get to growth.

# Selfless Selfish Self

Gave what was last in hand.
Gave a utopia.

A perfect need to others.
But what did that leave?

Exhausted.
No one understands how much sacrifice.

What lost thank you(s).
Lost sincerity goes unnoticed.

Selfless in nature.
Take back being selfish in love.

To not lose yourself.
To not let resentfulness seep into veins.

Testing the limits.
Perfection arriving at the door.

Worth will not wither.
Shining through the silver linings.

Extending grace to oneself.
Listening to one's heart.

# Slice of Hope

A sliver of hope can make all the difference.
Can shut out noises.

Pierce through hearts.
Screams the loudest in a dreary room.

Opens opportunity's door.
Waits for no human.

Slices through doubt.
Even if hope wavers.

# Urgent Calls

Watch firefighters rush to an emergency.
How blaring and alarming the sound makes

For a moment everything ceases.
Careens and swerves around the corner

Everyone lives and dies by a name.
What sacrifices that are made.

On the cusp of saving lives.
The cusp of urgency.

Once sat in the ocean.
Watch the seagulls gather fish.

Watch other people play with water.
In that moment soothed the specks of sand

How both calls to be at attention.
To be ever present.

# Calling Card

Hello. Hi. How are you?
Come again? Can not hear you?

Names scribbled.
A catalog of whom is to be remembered.

When a connection sparks a new tomorrow.
The extra effort in care.

The synergy held beyond gratitude.
The hope in building a future.

# Impact of Dynamics

Kinder, more gentler
Supportive and loving

Nurturing the wounds of untold stories.
A friend, a parent, a coach.

Sometimes in the forms of attempting.
Attempting to unlearn traumas.

Attempting to be healthier, wiser.
A strong sense of what gifts catapult into other's lives.

A strong sense of what success means.
To each it is something different.

Energizing an essential nutrient.
Nourishing self-compassion.

Living your whole truth.
Living and growing.

# Reawaken

It has always been the little things.
The little wonders of Earth.

Shaping and carving out experiences.
The little ones that make an everlasting experience.

Just a reminder to mold little experiences.
With ones that care.

With the ones that show a better world.
And in it can seem indulgent.

But indulge.
Indulge in what relationships foster.

A sense of awakening.
What a luxurious feeling to have met a special person.

# Vulnerability

Never knew this feeling crashed with others.
Careening and taking hold.

Sending shockwaves across emotions.
Yet it is a good thing.

Lately honesty sat on the line.
Reserved to say to others.

But it took courage to be that way with oneself.
To know what works for one's life and what does not.

Now taking the driver's seat,
This is a big role to fill.

# Enough

Eyes sought refuge in cold clasp gems.
Grace came knocking.

But does destiny feel the same?
Does gentleness press against these spaces?

Suffering not what love could give.
But what wholeheartedly is in the hands of the future.

There is permission.
Permission to self.

Permission to love oneself.
Permission to be first.

Identifying one's own wants and needs.
Setting boundaries.

Once was lost in navigating.
Now found a path in assurance.

# Trying New Beginnings

Sees what works
Sees what does not work

Sees frustration
But in the end, clarity.

Not what it is supposed to be
But how it gets remembered

And with any new beginning,
There stays love and hope.

A light at the end
An ever presence

Worming its way into storms.
Spinning the opposite way.

Creating a different type of ruckus.
Blooms excitement

Never to be in folly.
But to take time and enjoy what is to come.

9 798836 259877